D1321342

Just the Facts

Drugs and Sport

Clive Gifford

www.heinemann.co.uk/library
Visit our website to find out more information about **Heinemann Library** books.

To order:
 Phone 44 (0) 1865 888066
 Send a fax to 44 (0) 1865 314091
 Visit the Heinemann Bookshop at www.heinemann.co.uk/library to browse our catalogue and order online.

Produced by Monkey Puzzle Media Ltd
Gissing's Farm, Fressingfield, Suffolk IP21 5SH, UK

First published in Great Britain by Heinemann Library, Halley Court, Jordan Hill, Oxford OX2 8EJ, part of Harcourt Education.
Heinemann is a registered trademark of Harcourt Education Ltd.

Editorial: Sarah Eason and Georga Godwin
Design: Mark Whitchurch
Picture Research: Sally Cole
Consultants: Michele Verroken and Allison Connell, UK Sport
Production: Edward Moore

Originated by Dot Gradations Ltd
Printed and bound in Hong Kong, China by
South China Printing Company

ISBN 0 431 16162 3
08 07 06 05 04
10 9 8 7 6 5 4 3 2 1

British Library Cataloguing in Publication Data
Gifford, Clive
Drugs and sport
362.2'9'088796
A full catalogue record for this book is available from the British Library.

Acknowledgements
The publishers would like to thank the following for permission to reproduce photographs:
Action Plus p. **37** (Y. Villaume/DPPI); Corbis pp. **4–5** (Dmitri Lundt), **7** (Mug Shots), **8**, **10** (Bettmann), **12** (Bettmann), **19** (Bettmann), **28** (Julien Hekimian), **30** (Michael Kevin Daly), **34–35** (Pete Saloutos), **48–49** (Tom Stewart); Digital Vision p. **50–51**; PA Photos pp. **4** (John Giles), **14–15** (John Giles), **16** (EPA), **21** (EPA), **22** (EPA), **23** (Chris Ison), **27** (EPA), **29** (EPA), **38** (EPA), **40** (EPA), **41** (EPA), **42** (Peter Jordan), **45** (EPA), **44–45** (Rosie Hallam); Popperfoto pp. **11**, **13** (Reuters); Rex Features pp. **24** (Agence DPPI), **33** (IBL); Science Photo Library pp. **17**, **25** (Tek Image), **31** (Tek Image), **39** (Geoff Tom), **47** (Mauro Fermariello).

Cover photograph reproduced with permission of Getty Images (Stone).

Every effort has been made to contact copyright holders of any material reproduced in this book. Any omissions will be rectified in subsequent printings if notice is given to the publishers.

Any words appearing in the text in bold, **like this**, are explained in the Glossary.

Contents

Introduction

Sport is played regularly by more than a billion people all over the world. People take part in sports to relax, to stay healthy and to enjoy the excitement and fun that sport can create. Yet for some athletes, sport is much more than a game. It is so deadly serious that they will risk breaking the law, breaking their sport's rules, harming their body and even risking their life in order to win. These risk-takers are sports men and women who practise doping – taking banned drugs or using prohibited methods to **enhance** their performance.

US sprinter Maurice Greene celebrates his win at the 2000 Olympics. Athletes are under great pressure to succeed — over 100,000 people watched the race live and hundreds of millions followed it on TV.

“Sport is about health and honesty. Taking drugs is unhealthy and dishonest.”

Sir Arthur Gold, Chairman of the British Olympic Association

Performance-enhancing drugs come in many different shapes and forms.

No one knows just how many athletes are taking drugs to improve their chances of winning, but estimates for drug-taking run into many thousands for professional stars and hundreds of thousands for amateur athletes. Most of the substances that athletes take are banned because medical research has shown that they can cause serious, and sometimes life-threatening, health problems.

As well as being dangerous, many of the drugs that athletes take are illegal, not just in sports but in the whole of society. Laws vary in every country, but most nations have laws about owning, using or providing certain drugs. In the UK, for example, illegal drugs are divided into three classes: A, B and C. Class A includes **heroin**, **LSD** and **cocaine**. Prison sentences are common for people found selling or owning Class A drugs.

Even if a drug can be legally used in one country, it may be banned by the organization which runs a particular sport. For example, it is not an offence in the USA, Australia or the UK to drink alcohol, so long as you are over a certain age, do not drink to excess and are not in charge of a motor vehicle. However, many sports, including fencing, shooting and motor racing, have banned competitors from competing with alcohol in their bodies. Taking a drug that is banned by the representatives of a sport is breaking one of the sport's rules. It is cheating, pure and simple. Yet many competitors still take the risk, making the use of drugs one of the biggest problems facing sport today.

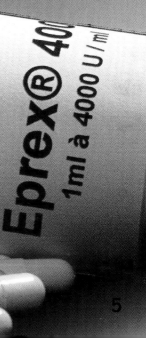

Why take drugs?

Athletes take drugs to help them improve their performance. This can be done in several ways. Some drugs help an athlete to recover from injury more rapidly. Other drugs can boost a person's strength, or improve their ability to train harder and for longer periods. Why do people turn to drugs if they are illegal, dangerous to health or against the rules of their sport? There are many reasons.

Sport has become big business, turning its most successful performers into multimillionaires, and bringing glory and celebrity status to the very best. Some competitors are desperate for a share of this fame and fortune and will consider anything that may help them to achieve it. Being a professional athlete is hard work and requires years of training, dedication and sacrifice. Yet, despite all this effort, only a handful of athletes can be winners. The difference between being first and coming second can be incredibly small – a fraction of a second or a handful of centimetres. With such a tiny margin between winning and losing, some are tempted to try anything that might give them the edge.

Under pressure

Athletes are under great pressure to succeed. This pressure comes from their team or club, from their family and friends and from their coaches and trainers. Most of all, the pressure can come from themselves. The desire to win must be very strong for an athlete to be successful. Careers in sport tend to be short, and competitors may only get one chance to become the very best. This pressure leads some competitors to turn to drugs so that they can make it to the biggest championships, beat their rivals or keep their place in the team. Further down the sporting ladder, the pressures to succeed are a little different but just as strong. Young athletes and other competitors see the stars in their sport as role models. If they think or know that their heroes are taking **performance-enhancing drugs**, they are more likely to follow their example.

Boxers who lose an important fight may never get the chance to compete at such a high level again. The pressure on them to win is enormous.

From ancient beginnings

Cycling was one of the first sports to pay its winners serious money. Here, a competitor prepares to start a race.

❝I would rather have won this race than be president of the USA.❞

Thomas Hicks, gold medallist in the 1904 Olympics marathon, who nearly died after the race

The use of drugs in sport is not new. Ever since organized sport began, there has been pressure on those who take part. The first known major sporting contests were the ancient Greek Olympics, which started in 776 BCE. By 400 BCE, the games were attracting large audiences and there were massive rewards for the winners. Prize money, free houses and food for life were common rewards for the athletes. Winners often paid no taxes and did not need to serve in armies. Many competitors consumed anything that might give them an advantage. Some even ate the **testicles** of dogs, goats or sheep in order to gain extra strength! Others ate certain types of wild mushroom, which contained powerful drugs. The ancient Romans enjoyed more bloodthirsty sports, including battles between **gladiators**. Many gladiators drank alcohol or took the drug opium to make them fight harder and to dull the pain.

The start of the modern era

Large sporting events declined after the fall of the Roman Empire, in the 5th century CE, and did not re-emerge until the 19th century. But once the sporting events had been established, it did not take long for the use of drugs to follow. In 1865, swimmers racing along the canals of the Dutch city of Amsterdam are believed to have taken a mixture of **heroin** and **cocaine**, two drugs which were not illegal at that time. Cycling was one of the first sports to pay its best competitors a living wage. Many long-distance cyclists from the 1880s onwards used wine mixed with cocaine as a way of overcoming pain and tiredness. The Welshman, Arthur Linton, tied for first place in the 1896 Bordeaux to Paris race, but shortly afterwards died of an overdose of the **stimulant** trimethyl, which he had taken to give him extra energy. He became the first recorded victim of drugs in sport. The modern Olympic Games started the same year that Linton died and in 1904 the Games were held in the American city of St Louis. The winner of the men's marathon race, Thomas Hicks, collapsed very soon after the race and only long hours of struggle by doctors saved his life. During the race, Hicks' trainers had fed him brandy and a mixture containing the whites of eggs and the drug **strychnine**. Strychnine was believed to act as a stimulant, but it is also a powerful poison which is used today to kill rats. Hicks never ran another race.

The rise in drug use

Drug use in sport continued in the 20th century even after substances like **heroin** and **cocaine** were made illegal in many countries. Scientific researchers developed new drugs, such as **amphetamines**, that increased alertness, made the heart beat faster and reduced feelings of tiredness. They also discovered ways of making certain substances found in the human body, such as **testosterone** (see page 17). Testosterone was given to some German soldiers during World War II to make them more aggressive. After the war, some of the German scientists who had worked on the testosterone programme turned to sport, helping athletics coaches in the Soviet Union and the countries of Eastern Europe. Athletes there began to use drugs such as testosterone to build up their muscles in order to give themselves more strength, power and **stamina**. Soviet and East German athletes started to win many competitions and, in response, the USA developed **anabolic steroids**, which boost muscle growth. In the 1960s, steroids found their way into athletics, American football and other power sports.

In 1960, the Soviet athletes Tamara and Irina Press became the first sisters to win gold medals at the same Olympics. Questions remain over whether they had taken testosterone.

The need for 'speed'

In the 1930s, a new kind of drug, called amphetamine, was developed. Intended to treat colds and hay fever, it was found to have other effects on the body, which earned it the nickname of 'speed'. The drug kept people awake, made the heart beat faster and the brain work more rapidly. After World War II, amphetamines were heavily used by cyclists, speed skaters and other athletes, who wanted a speed advantage no matter what the cost. And the cost proved very high for Knud Jensen, a 23-year-old Danish cyclist. Jensen died from an overdose of amphetamines an hour after competing in a race at the 1960 Olympics.

Seven years later, another cyclist, Britain's Tommy Simpson, died of an amphetamine overdose. Competing in the 1967 Tour de France, Simpson was on a steep mountain road in blazing temperatures. In front of a large television audience, he collapsed, and was helped back on to his bike only to collapse again and die. The amphetamines he had taken combined with heat exhaustion to cause his heart to fail.

❝I would argue that a huge percentage of world records broken in the last 30 years were drug-assisted.❞

Chuck Yesalis, Professor of Health and Human Development, Penn State University, USA

British cyclist, Tommy Simpson, takes a bend in the 1962 Tour de France. Five years later, he collapsed and died while he was competing in the Tour de France.

International action

Up until the 1960s, little was done to stop the use of drugs in sport. Most sports organizations turned a blind eye to drug use. Deaths, illnesses and increasing concerns eventually led to changes, but they took a long time to come. In 1963, France became the first country to make new laws against doping in sport. Tommy Simpson's death in 1967 finally forced the International Olympic Committee (IOC), the organization which runs the Olympics, to take action. They set up a Medical Commission, which started to produce a list of banned substances, and began drugs testing at the 1968 Mexico Olympics. Testing became more common throughout the 1970s and 1980s, but many athletes simply skipped testing rather than risk being caught. In 1983, at the Pan American Games, seventeen competitors from Cuba, Canada, the USA and many other nations were found to have used prohibited **performance-enhancing drugs**. Many more athletes left the games to avoid being tested. New testing methods and stronger punishments were introduced in the mid-1980s, but these could not stop tragedies from happening, such as the case of Birgit Dressel.

Champion US hammer-thrower, Harold Connolly, shows off his Olympic gold medal. In 1973, Connolly said: 'The overwhelming majority of athletes I know would do anything short of killing themselves to improve athletic performance'.

Case study Birgit Dressel

The West German athlete, Birgit Dressel, looked healthy and strong, and was a possible future winner of an Olympic gold medal. In 1986, she had won fourth place in the seven-event **heptathlon** of the European Athletics Championships. However, Dressel's body was a wreck from years of taking prohibited drugs, including **steroids**, to boost her performance. On 8 April 1987, while practising the shot put, Dressel felt pain in her left hip and buttocks. Over the next two days she saw more than 20 medical specialists as the pain grew in intensity. Her heart was racing, her fingers turned blue and her kidneys and liver began to fail. She was rushed into a hospital intensive-care unit, where doctors gave her oxygen and changed her entire blood four times, but all was in vain. She died in agony on 10 April 1987.

West German athlete, Birgit Dressel, prepares to throw a javelin in the seven-event heptathlon in 1986. Less than a year later she was dead.

13

Prohibited substances and methods

To tackle the issue of drugs in sport, the authorities responsible for different sports have drawn up lists of drugs and methods of taking them which are prohibited (banned) in their sport. Many sports authorities base their lists on the International Olympic Committee Medical Commission and World Anti-Doping Agency list. This is split into three parts: prohibited substances, prohibited methods and substances that are prohibited in certain circumstances.

Prohibited substances

Substances are banned in sport because of their potential to **enhance** an athlete's performance artificially and also because of the risks they pose to an athlete's health and to the safety of other competitors. Prohibited substances include classes of drugs such as **anabolic steroids** (see page 17) and **diuretics** (see page 23).

Prohibited methods

Prohibited methods include **blood doping**, in which extra blood is added to an athlete's body shortly before a competition (see page 24). In 2003, a new method called gene doping was added to the list of prohibited methods. By using this method, athletes may alter their genes (the parts of a body's cells that determine how big or strong a person is) – removing their weaker genes and building up the potential of their stronger genes.

Prohibited substances in certain circumstances

Some classes of drug are not banned in all sports. These substances include alcohol, cannabis, **local anaesthetics** and **beta-blockers**. The international governing body for each sport has the authority to decide whether these kinds of substance should be prohibited in their sport.

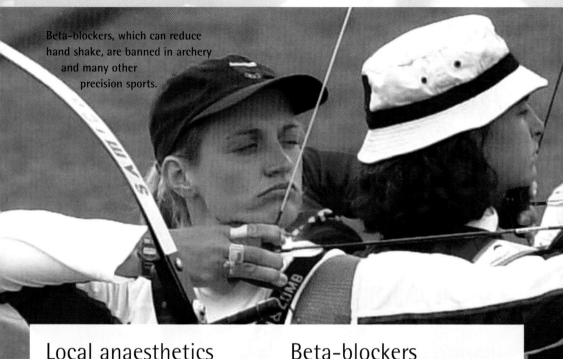

Beta-blockers, which can reduce hand shake, are banned in archery and many other precision sports.

Local anaesthetics

A local anaesthetic is a substance that produces a loss of feeling in an area of the body for a short time. Some local anaesthetics are injected by doctors and dentists as painkillers before they operate. They are also found in small quantities in syrups used to treat sore throats and other medicines sold in stores. Local anaesthetics are not completely banned, because they could be used to remove pain from an injury so that an athlete can continue to train or perform. Many sports only allow certain local anaesthetics to be injected by a doctor but insist that the sport's governing body is notified about these treatments.

Beta-blockers

Beta-blockers cause the heart to slow down the rate at which it pumps blood around the body, reducing high blood pressure and helping to prevent heart attacks. Beta-blockers also calm the body and reduce tremors or shakes, giving the athlete a steady hand. They are prohibited in snooker, where they would give a competitor an unfair advantage, but they are not banned in sports like athletics, where they could actually slow an athlete down. Athletes without a heart problem who take beta-blockers are at risk from tiredness, breathing difficulties and even heart failure.

Steroids

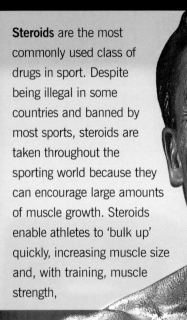

Steroids are the most commonly used class of drugs in sport. Despite being illegal in some countries and banned by most sports, steroids are taken throughout the sporting world because they can encourage large amounts of muscle growth. Steroids enable athletes to 'bulk up' quickly, increasing muscle size and, with training, muscle strength, enabling them to train harder and longer. These gains, though, come at a high cost. Taking steroids tampers seriously with the chemistry of the human body. They can lead to large-scale and harmful changes, which are hard or even impossible to reverse.

Singaporean Sazali Samad wins a 2002 bodybuilding championship. Other bodybuilders have used steroids to boost muscle growth.

Anabolic androgenic steroids

Anabolic androgenic steroids (or **anabolic steroids** for short) resemble substances called **hormones** made in the human body, but they are synthetic (made in laboratories rather than occurring naturally). Most anabolic steroids resemble the hormone **testosterone**, which is produced in the **testicles** of men and, to a lesser extent, in the **ovaries** of women.

Androgenic means 'making masculine' and anabolic means 'building up'. Anabolic androgenic steroids work with the hormone testosterone to help produce male sexual characteristics and stimulate the growth of bones and muscles. Steroids are injected or taken by mouth to raise the levels of testosterone or similar hormones in the blood. Steroid users may experience muscle growth, more aggressive and competitive emotions and shorter recovery times after injury.

Steroid use started in power sports like weightlifting, American football and the throwing events in athletics, but it quickly spread into a large range of sports from rugby and tennis to baseball and swimming. In 1998, for example, three Chinese swimmers, one just fifteen years old, were banned for four years because they used anabolic steroids.

Steroids are rarely available without a medical **prescription** but most athletes who use them find other ways to obtain a supply. They are found in certain health or bodybuilding supplements that are available from shops or for sale via newspaper ads or the Internet. A large **black market** worth millions of pounds exists for trading illegally in steroids.

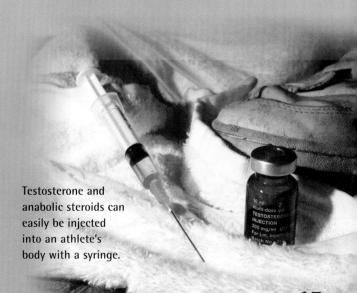

Testosterone and anabolic steroids can easily be injected into an athlete's body with a syringe.

The dangers of steroids

The ways that **steroids** can influence an individual's physical growth and personality are not fully understood. However, it is known that steroids have many far-reaching side effects. Some side effects happen early on and include swollen feet, high blood pressure and **acne** on the face, back and neck.

Steroid users have many extra **hormones** in their blood, and these all need to be broken down by the liver. The increased level of hormones that the liver has to deal with can cause major damage. The kidneys and heart can also be permanently harmed through regular steroid use. Steroids can damage the development of a child or young teenager, causing their growth to be stopped or stunted. Steroids can also affect the user's personality. Many steroid users experience intense bouts of aggression, which can spill over into violence. This aggression is common enough to have its own nickname: 'roid rage'.

Steroids can make changes to a person's sexual characteristics. Males may develop breasts and lose body hair. Their **testicles** may shrivel up and they may become unable to produce sperm. Women may start to develop baldness, facial hair and a deepening of their voice. Their breasts may reduce in size, their periods may become irregular or stop and their genitals may enlarge.

Case study

Lyle Alzado

After winning 27 fights as an amateur boxer, Lyle Alzado became an American football star playing defence for the Denver Broncos, Cleveland Browns and the LA Raiders, with whom he won a superbowl championship. After retiring, he acted in movies and owned a restaurant in Hollywood. It appeared that he was having the sort of life that many people dream about. Alzado, however, had been taking steroids since the age of 22 and was in constant agony. Before his death at the age of 42 from brain cancer brought on by steroid use, Alzado went public and admitted: 'I became violent on the field and off it. I did things only crazy people do. Now look at me. My hair's gone, I wobble when I walk and I have trouble remembering things. My last wish? That no one else ever dies this way.'

American footballer Lyle Alzado was a sporting superstar and a budding film actor before steroids helped to cause his early death.

Stimulants

After **steroids**, **stimulants** are the second most common drug found by testing in sports. Many different drugs are stimulants, including **amphetamines** and **cocaine**. Even caffeine, which is found in coffee, tea and many fizzy drinks, is a dangerous stimulant when taken in large doses, especially when it is combined with physical exercise.

Stimulants force the lungs and heart to work faster, moving blood more quickly around the body and making the brain work more rapidly. As a result, users feel less tired and more alert. Athletes who have taken stimulants admit to feeling more confident and more aggressive and can sometimes hold the belief that they are unbeatable.

Stimulants do not create energy. In fact, they take energy from the body and, as the drug's effects fade, users can feel exhausted, depressed and anxious. The positive sensations caused by stimulants and the negative feelings afterwards help to make these drugs **addictive**. Stimulants can cause heart problems and high blood pressure. When training or competing in high temperatures, stimulants can cause further problems, leading to heat exhaustion and death. This was the case with the cyclist, Tommy Simpson (see page 11).

Russian figure skaters Anton Sikharulidze and Elena Berezhnaya were forced to withdraw from the World Figure Skating Championships when Berezhnaya tested positive for a banned stimulant.

Over the counter

Certain stimulants, such as amphetamines, are illegal, while others are banned in sports but can still be bought freely in shops. **Ephedrine** is an example of one such drug. In many countries, including the USA, ephedrine is sold in health-food stores as a weight-loss or energy-boosting food supplement.

Athletes may deliberately avoid buying ephedrine but they have to be incredibly careful over any food supplement, drink or medicine they take. This is because stimulants are found in a surprisingly large number of everyday items. Sometimes as little as two cups of freshly-brewed regular coffee, for example, can be enough to cause an athlete to fail a drugs test.

Ephedrine and other stimulants are found in many medicines, including cold remedies and hay fever medicines. These have caused many **positive drugs tests** in sports as varied as American football and downhill skiing. In 2001, the 100-metre and 200-metre sprinter, Ato Bolden, tested positive for ephedrine, which was traced back to a cough medicine he had taken. In 2000, the world champion pairs figure skater, Elena Berezhnaya, became the first ever female figure skater to test positive for a banned substance – her medicine for bronchitis, bought on a doctor's advice, contained a banned stimulant.

Narcotic analgesics and diuretics

Some cyclists use narcotic analgesics to allow them to compete in gruelling races even though they are badly injured.

Every home's medicine cabinet contains **analgesics**, such as paracetamol, aspirin and other common painkillers. **Narcotic analgesics**, which include **morphine**, **methadone** and **heroin**, are much stronger and far more dangerous. They act on the brain and the central **nervous system** to suppress or reduce the amount of pain felt by a person.

In medicine, narcotic analgesics are used to remove some of the agony suffered by terminally-ill patients. In sports, some athletes have turned to narcotic analgesics because these drugs allow them to compete even with a serious injury. But not only do they risk making their injury permanent, they also open the door to these drugs' lethal side effects. Narcotic analgesics can cause vomiting, depression and serious breathing and heart problems. Taken in excess, they can cause a person to go into a coma or die. What makes them even more dangerous is that they are highly **addictive**. A person can quickly become **dependent** on doses of such a drug and, with regular use, a **tolerance** to the drug builds up. This means that people have to use more of the substance to obtain the same effect.

Diuretics

Some sports, including boxing, judo, weightlifting and rowing, have strict weight categories within which athletes compete. To make sure that they weigh the correct amount for their weight category, some competitors may misuse a prohibited class of drug called **diuretics**.

Diuretics act on the kidneys to produce more urine and remove fluids from the body quickly, reducing an athlete's weight. However, diuretics can remove too much water from the body, leading to **dehydration**. This can cause dizziness, headaches, cramps and loss of balance. At its most serious, it can cause both the kidneys and the heart to fail.

Diuretic drugs are a great temptation for jockeys, who have to keep their weight below a certain limit.

In sports with weight categories, tests for diuretics in competitors' urine are regularly carried out. At the 2000 Olympics, Izabela Dragneva, the first ever female weightlifting gold medallist, was found to have used diuretics and was stripped of her gold medal. Two of her Bulgarian countrymen, Ivan Ivanov and Sevdalin Minchev, also lost Olympic medals for using diuretics.

Diuretics can also be used for another purpose in sports. They increase the amount of urine produced, and so they may be used to dilute traces in the urine of other banned drugs, such as **steroids**. Because of this function as a possible **masking agent**, diuretics are prohibited in all sports.

Oxygen-increasing drugs

Muscles need oxygen in order to perform, and getting extra oxygen to an athlete's muscles can boost their performance. Training for months at high altitude where there is less oxygen in the air is one legal way of increasing the amount of oxygen that reaches an athlete's muscles. However, there are other ways which are banned in sports and create health risks. **Blood doping** and EPO are two banned methods.

Members of the Festina cycling team face the press. The team was kicked out of the 1998 Tour de France after large amounts of EPO were found in their possession.

Blood doping

In the past, the most common method of boosting oxygen levels artificially was blood doping. This involved taking some of an athlete's blood weeks or months before a sports event, letting the body replace the missing blood naturally and then injecting extra blood, complete with extra oxygen-carrying **haemoglobin**, shortly before competition. Blood doping carries health risks, including infections and the risk of blood clots. It can also cause heart failure as the extra blood is forced round the body, putting extra pressure on the heart. Blood doping is banned from competition sports.

EPO

In the 1980s there came word of a new 'wonder drug' for doping cheats which did all that blood doping could do and much more. The drug was, in fact, a substance which is produced naturally by the kidneys and regulates how many red blood cells appear in the blood. Known as EPO (short for erythropoietin), it is valuable in medicine, where it is used to treat patients suffering a shortage of red blood cells. Taken by people with normal red-blood-cell counts, EPO can increase the thickness of the blood so much that it can cause blood clotting and heart attacks.

A number of cyclists are believed to have died due to EPO but, because it has been hard to test for, no one can be certain. For athletes in endurance sports, injecting EPO may carry health risks, but it has been proved to boost performance by as much as twelve to fifteen per cent – a massive amount. For this reason, it is believed to be widespread in cycling and also in long-distance running. In some sports, athletes are given a urine test for EPO, while other sports authorities insist on a blood test as well as a urine test.

Increasing oxygen uptake

The ability of muscles to use oxygen is known as oxygen uptake. During intense exercise, oxygen gets used up and the body cannot supply enough oxygen to the muscles. This creates tiredness and stops muscles performing at their peak. Around 97 per cent of oxygen reaching muscles is carried by haemoglobin found in red blood cells. Increasing the amount of haemoglobin in an athlete's body can increase the oxygen uptake by muscles. This is what happens when athletes train at high altitudes, when they practise blood doping or they take EPO.

A laboratory technician filters out white blood cells from donated blood.

Recreational drugs

Some drugs do not **enhance** performance, but are still taken by athletes away from competition to help them relax or to give them a 'buzz'. These sorts of substances are known as **recreational drugs**. Alcohol, cannabinoids, which include **marijuana** and **hashish**, and some **stimulants** are used as recreational drugs.

Relaxants

Alcohol and cannabinoids are classed as relaxants because they dull the activity of the brain and a person's **nervous system**. They rarely improve an athlete's performance and can cause people to lose their balance, as well as reducing their sharpness of vision and affecting their ability to make judgements. Some people become addicted to alcohol and regular, heavy use can cause liver failure and other serious health problems.

Alcohol and cannabinoids are taken by many people in order to relax and remove tension, even though they can be prohibited by a sport and are illegal in some societies. The American world-record holding sprint swimmer, Gary Hall Junior, was found to have smoked marijuana at the 1996 Olympics. At that time, the drug was not on the list of banned substances in swimming and Hall only got a warning. Two years later, he again tested positive for marijuana, was banned for three months and was fined US$8000.

Different responses

Sports authorities respond differently to the use of recreational drugs by their participants. In soccer, especially in the past, alcohol was part of the off-pitch lifestyle of many European players and little action was taken. Some players, including George Best and Tony Adams, became addicted to alcohol. In contrast, the authorities in motorsports such as racing, rallying and motorbiking take recreational drug use very seriously. Few competitors use recreational drugs before racing as they dull reactions and judgement, but in 1997 the first positive test for marijuana led to Australian Anthony Gobert being banned from motorcycling.

Some sports have banned certain recreational drugs while turning a blind eye to others. In the USA, the National Basketball Association (NBA) banned **cocaine** after a period during the 1970s and 1980s when up to half of its players were believed to have used the drug. Marijuana is frowned upon but not actually banned.

In 2002, the winner of the Formula 3000 motor racing championship, Tomas Enge, tested positive for the drug cannabis.

In October 2002 he was stripped of his 2002 championship title and was given a suspended twelve-month ban from motor racing.

The Argentinian soccer star, Diego Maradona, was suspended for fifteen months in 1991, after testing positive for cocaine.

Drugs testing

There are a number of ways in which the issue of drugs in sport is being tackled, including educating athletes to stay drug-free. One of the most important ways of tackling the problem is to catch those using drugs and punish them. Testing for use of banned drugs or methods of enhancing performance started at the 1968 Olympics and has become a major field of research and debate.

The most common form of testing is the urine test. In most major sports events, the athletes in first, second and third places are each tested, and then further competitors are picked at random. An athlete is instructed to provide a urine sample which is divided into two, an A and a B sample, by the athlete under the supervision of the Doping Control Officer (DCO). These samples go to a laboratory for analysis and the results are sent back to the anti-doping agency responsible for conducting the test and to the governing body of the sport.

At the laboratory, technicians use special equipment to separate the various substances that make up the A sample, and then identify what each substance is and how much of it is contained within the sample. Many banned drugs, including **anabolic steroids** and **stimulants** such as **amphetamines** can be detected from

French technicians at the National Drug Testing Centre test athletes' urine for traces of EPO.

a sample of the athlete's urine. If an athlete's A sample tests positive for a banned substance, but the athlete challenges this result, then the B sample may be tested in front of the athlete and a person of their choice. If either or both samples are positive, the athlete is asked to attend a hearing of their case. This hearing is usually held by a disciplinary group of the sport in question. Athletes who refuse to give samples for testing or are shown to have tampered with their sample are considered to have given a positive test and are asked to explain the reasons for their actions.

Setting a limit

Many substances occur naturally in the body or can be taken in small amounts with no harm or performance-enhancing benefit. Sports authorities set a limit above which it is considered that the drugs test is positive. However, problems occur with setting these limits for different drugs. If the limit is too high, an athlete could still enjoy unfair performance-enhancing benefits from a drug. If it is too low, drugs which occur naturally in the body in small amounts could possibly provide a positive result in a drugs test. The disputed cases of athletes testing positive for **nandrolone** (see page 43) show the controversy that this can cause.

Italian cyclist, Marco Pantani, was convicted of using a banned substance in 2000, but has always disputed his test results.

❝We were the first organization fighting doping. We won many battles, but we did not win the war.❞

Former head of the International Olympic Committee [IOC], Juan Antonio Samaranch

29

A cat-and-mouse game

At first, drugs testing was primitive and not carefully policed and it only took place at competitions. Some drug users managed to fool testers by swapping urine samples or switching to new drugs which were not banned. Others learned quickly that they could avoid testing positive by stopping using banned drugs weeks before the event. They still received benefits from drugs such as **steroids**, which helped them to build muscle in training, but tested negative at the competition and got away with drug misuse.

One way that the anti-doping forces have fought back is by introducing random, out-of-competition testing. This is where a drugs-testing official arrives unannounced at an athlete's training camp or home. The athlete must then give a urine sample in view of the tester. This surprise method is used because some drugs cheats have been found to keep samples of 'clean' urine in containers taped to their bodies. Some athletes protest at the inconvenience of being contacted at any time and being ordered to take a drugs test. Other critics point to the high cost of performing hundreds and thousands of random tests every year. Yet, 'knock and pee' tests, as they are nicknamed, are considered a major step forward in catching cheats. They also act as a **deterrent** to those athletes thinking about starting to use drugs.

Sometimes, a drugs testing official arrives unannounced while athletes are training or practising at home.

Advances on both sides

In the 1980s, new and more accurate testing equipment was developed, and testing became more strictly controlled. Yet, as testing methods have advanced, so have ways of cheating. Some athletes have switched to new **performance-enhancing drugs**, such as **creatine**, which are not yet banned. Others use drugs which can help hide or mask the effects of taking a banned drug. In some cases, athletes have turned to banned drugs, like the human growth **hormone**, which reduces body fat and boosts muscles, because no accepted, reliable test has yet been introduced for it.

The cat-and-mouse game continues with anti-doping authorities funding research into new tests for human growth hormone and more accurate testing for substances like EPO and steroids. The development of a machine called an isotope ratio mass spectrometer, for instance, may mean that tests can spot the difference between naturally-produced **testosterone** and testosterone created by banned substances injected into the body.

A selection of sealed testing kits for a range of different drugs including amphetamines, heroin and cocaine.

31

Punishing offenders

Sports authorities call punishments 'sanctions'. They decide on what sanctions to deliver to a guilty athlete based on the type of substance or method used, the number of times the competitor has been tested positive and the regulations in their sport.

An athlete who fails a drugs test is usually sent home from a competition. If a **positive drugs test** occurs after they have taken part in a competition, guilty athletes usually lose their place in the record books and any medals or prize money they have collected.

Sporting bodies can hand out fines, but the main sanction is to ban an athlete from competing in their sport for any length of time from three months through to life. In Olympic competition, any athlete found guilty of drug offences is given a two-year ban if it is their first offence and a lifetime ban for a second offence. In 2001, the organization which runs world swimming, FINA, gave a lifetime ban to Greek swimmer, Vasileios Demetis, after he failed his second drugs test.

Guilty athletes often face further punishments in the form of losing money from **sponsors**. They also find that money-making appearances as a celebrity often disappear. Recently, several countries, such as France and Italy, have made many of the drugs used in sport illegal throughout the whole of society. This means that those who take illegal drugs in sport may face criminal charges, fines and imprisonment.

> **❝I believe that if you get caught on drugs, you should get a lifetime ban. There's no need for you in our sport, and there's no room for you in our sport.❞**
>
> Champion sprinter, Maurice Greene

Case study Ben Johnson

Ben Johnson became the world's fastest man when he clocked 9.79 seconds in the 100-metre race at the 1988 Olympics. Days later, he was stripped of his gold medal and world record after testing positive for a **steroid** called stanozolol. Johnson received a two-year ban from the International Association of Athletics Federations (IAAF) and then a lifetime ban when he tested positive again in 1993. Johnson went from sprint king to disgraced ex-champion. He lost the respect of many athletics fans and millions of dollars in sponsorship. In 1999, the Canadian courts let Johnson race in his own country, but the IAAF upheld his ban which meant anyone racing against him would be banned themselves. A once-great champion was forced to race against animals and cars.

Ben Johnson wins the 1988 Olympic 100-metre final, smashing the world record in the process. Days later, he was in disgrace.

Organization and education

A coach encourages his junior soccer team. Coaches can help educate young sportspeople about the dangers of taking drugs.

Sport is an international business, with athletes globetrotting around the world to train and compete in all continents. Keeping a record of where athletes are and how and when they have been tested can be difficult. Many countries have organizations dedicated to drugs testing and fighting drugs in sport. In some countries, bodies governing individual sports are in control of fighting drug-taking amongst their own participants. This leads to an enormous number of different groups.

To keep track of the athletes and the work of the many different anti-drugs organizations, sports are getting more organized and working together. In 1999, following the World Conference on Doping, the World Anti-Doping Agency (**WADA**) was created. This organization is designed to help coordinate the work of the many different bodies so that they can, together, fund new research and share knowledge on new drugs and forms of testing.

Over time, WADA may begin to influence sports organizations to agree on the same sets of rules for doping. Many people feel that if all sports organizations could agree on the same drugs and testing codes, it would be much easier for the media to get the anti-doping message across to the public.

Education

Getting more organized will not solve the doping problem by itself. Education is vital in helping both young and established athletes to avoid using drugs in sport. Some education programmes in schools, colleges and sports clubs concentrate on the harm that drugs can do to an athlete's health, the punishments for being caught or the pride and success one can achieve by competing without using drugs. Other initiatives target coaches, parents, teachers and sports fans to spot signs of potential doping and to place less pressure on athletes to succeed by taking drugs.

Banned substances are found in hundreds and thousands of different foods, drinks, supplements and medicines. Many education schemes use telephone hotlines, computer databases and Internet websites to advise athletes and their coaches about testing rules and where banned substances appear. At the 2002 **Commonwealth Games** for instance, a medical pharmacy was built in the athletes' village. The pharmacy staff were specially trained and could supply competitors and coaches with anti-doping information.

Helping their own sport

Many people feel that the organizations that run sports can only do so much and that more needs to be done by participants in the sports. Athletes can declare themselves drug-free, donate time and money to educate others and use their great influence to promote anti-doping.

WADA's new Athletes' Passport scheme is one way in which athletes can help. Athletes voluntarily join the scheme and promise to submit to drugs testing. The passport gives them updated information on banned drugs and methods and contains a complete record of all their testing. It also acts as a declaration of their drug-free status. Over 700 athletes joined WADA's athletes' scheme at its introduction at the 2002 Winter Olympics.

Sports stars' influence

In 1998, baseball's Mark McGuire set a record for the most home runs hit in a season. He then admitted that he had been using a **steroid** substitute, which was allowed in baseball but banned in most other sports. Sales of the steroid substitute soared and disapproval of steroids dropped amongst young people. This sort of influence is the reason why top sports stars are paid large amounts to promote products such as computer games, cereals and clothing. It is also the reason why such athletes are the focus of many anti-doping campaigns.

Some anti-drugs schemes involve talking to top athletes and making it clear that they have a responsibility as role models to sports fans and young athletes. In athletics, one campaign calls for athletes to wear a red ribbon on their vests to make it clear that they are drug-free. Other campaigns use champions to promote anti-doping messages to other athletes and young people in general. The US National Youth Anti-Drug Media Campaign, for example, features sports stars including Venus and Serena Williams on TV adverts, posters and billboards.

Some athletes chose to go it alone and make public their anti-drugs views. British **decathlete** Daley Thompson was an outspoken critic of drugs use in world athletics in the 1980s and 1990s. Today, Ian Thorpe, the world's most famous swimmer, often uses his celebrity to call for tougher punishments for drugs cheats. At the World Athletics Championships in 2001, runner Paula Radcliffe protested against certain runners who had allegedly taken the banned drug, EPO. Her sign reading: 'EPO Cheats Out' grabbed the attention of the world's media.

Young French demonstrators hold up a home-made syringe to protest against drug use in the Tour de France.

Stopping the doping trade

Stopping drugs from reaching athletes is a complex and difficult task because the drugs come from many sources. Some athletes who seek out illegal drugs such as **cocaine** and **heroin** may come into contact with criminal drugs rings. Large **black markets** exist for supplying **steroids** and other banned **performance-enhancing drugs** to athletes or their coaches. A number of athletes obtain drugs from their doctors, using **prescriptions**. In many cases, the doctors are unaware that they are supplying a medication that is banned in the sport that their patient plays.

The case of Manfred Ewald

Manfred Ewald leaves the court in Germany after being found guilty of doping young athletes.

❝It was terrifying what they did to us. I took up to 30 pills a day. They always told us they were vitamins. There was no question you would not take them.❞

Carola Beraktschjan, former East German world-record-holding swimmer testifying at the trial of Manfred Ewald

In some cases, drugs have been supplied, not by a coach, but by a country's official sports body. In East Germany, from the 1960s onwards, athletes were ordered to take part in a doping programme organized by Manfred Ewald, the head of the country's Olympic athletics programme. In July 2000, Ewald was found guilty of doping more than 100 sportswomen, some as young as eleven. While he was in charge, East Germany, which has a population of just 17 million, won a staggering 160 Olympic gold medals. Many of the athletes who were doped suffered health problems for years afterwards.

Educating doctors is very important, as many of them may not be aware of all the substances that are banned in sports.

Stronger punishments

Anti-doping authorities work closely with the police and other agencies to track down and catch people who supply drugs to athletes. They also press governments to introduce tougher laws and punishments. In some countries, such as the USA, the supply of steroids for non-medical uses is illegal. Former British athlete, David Jenkins, was given a seven-year jail sentence when he was found guilty of smuggling more than US$70-million worth of steroids across the border from Mexico to the USA. Ten years later, Willy Vogt, a team trainer with the Festina Tour De France cycling team, was jailed for possession of large amounts of the banned drug, EPO. In France, Vogt's actions were a crime, but in other countries, such as the UK, they are only against the rules of the sport. Anti-doping authorities want to see stricter laws introduced in all countries to make supplying performance-enhancing drugs just as serious an offence as supplying dangerous **recreational drugs** such as cocaine and heroin.

Are all drug takers cheats?

Some athletes, such as Ben Johnson, first claim that they are innocent. Only at a later point do they, or their coach or doctor, admit to them taking illegal drugs. Such cases reinforce the view of many people that positive tests for banned drugs show an athlete to be guilty and a drug cheat. The truth is not always quite so simple. Drug tests are not foolproof and mistakes can occur. Some athletes who are first labelled as cheats are later cleared when it is found that there was an error in testing. For example, sprinter Merlene Ottey's two-year ban was overturned when it was found that a laboratory had not tested her urine sample properly. In an attempt to make the drug tests as accurate as possible, an international standard has been established and sports organizations can be awarded a certificate by the International Standards Organization.

Jamaican sprinter Merlene Ottey's ban for taking an anabolic steroid was lifted in 2000, when a panel decided there was a lack of evidence.

Inadvertent doping

Inadvertent doping occurs when an athlete takes a drink, food or medicine without realizing that it contains a banned substance. The sprinter, Ato Bolden, rugby players such as Australia's Ben Tune and tennis player Petr Korda all claimed to have taken food, drink or medicines without realizing that they contained a prohibited substance. As a result, they returned **positive drugs tests**. Sometimes, when athletes plead that they have inadvertently taken a doping substance, no **sanctions** are imposed or a much shorter ban is given.

Many people feel that ignorance should be no defence and that professional athletes should know exactly what they are consuming. There is plenty of advice available from experts, databases on the Internet and telephone hotlines run by sports organizations. When drugs are such a major issue, shouldn't athletes take responsibility for exactly what goes into their bodies?

Some people inside sport argue that it is hard to check absolutely everything that an athlete eats. There is also the additional issue of spiking – when a competitor's food, drink, medicine or even their drugs-test sample has a banned drug added to it without their knowing. The intention of spiking is usually to make the athlete fail a drugs test. Many athletes claim that spiking has occurred, but few of these claims can be proved. In 1993, the Russian hurdler, Lyudmila Narozhilenko (now Lyudmila Enquist) was banned for four years after testing positive for **anabolic steroids**. In 1995, the ban was lifted when her husband admitted to spiking her food with steroids in a fit of jealousy after she had asked him for a divorce.

The Australian rugby player Ben Tune (right) escaped punishment when he admitted to using a banned drug to treat a knee injury.

41

Legal battles

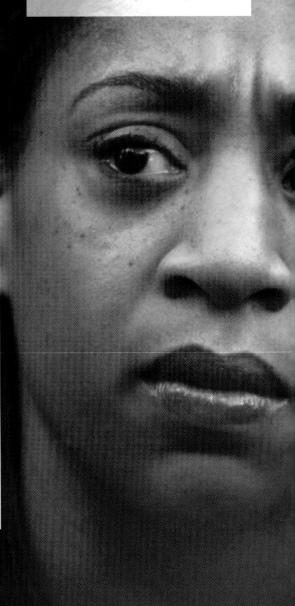

Imagine being a world champion one day and then labelled a 'drugs cheat' the next! Some athletes who test positive feel shame and fear because they have deliberately drugged their bodies and have been caught. Others feel confused or angry, as they seriously believe that they have done nothing wrong.

The results of drug tests are often questioned by the athlete and their coach, and this usually leads to a court case. This can be an expensive business and take a long time to be resolved. In 1992, the British 800-metre runner, Diane Modahl, was tested positive for drugs and banned from running. Four years later, the test was found to be faulty and the ban was lifted. Modahl then claimed compensation for the time she had been wrongly banned from running. Eventually, in 2001, a judge finally ruled that she had lost her appeal. As court cases like this rumble on, the negative image of drugs and doping hangs over both the athlete and the sport that they take part in.

Diane Modahl leaves the High Court in London, after losing her case for damages for the ban which stopped her from competing for four years.

Are the sports authorities doing enough? The International Olympic Committee recently spent several million pounds on new research for drugs testing. However, critics say that as sport generates billions rather than millions of pounds, a great deal more still needs to be spent. Foolproof drugs tests would act as a stronger **deterrent** to athletes considering drugs as an option. Better tests would also remove confusion about results and reduce the number of court cases that occur.

The case of nandrolone

Nandrolone is a banned **anabolic steroid** which is a close chemical cousin of **testosterone**. Recently, a number of athletes have tested positive for nandrolone, including the British sprinter, Linford Christie, and the French soccer player, Christophe Dugarry. New medical studies have since shown that a small amount of nandrolone can naturally occur in the human body and this amount might be raised by the stresses that athletes put on their body. Further research has shown that the body may convert legal, unbanned substances into nandrolone.

In 1999, the sports organization UK Sport set up a committee of experts to look at the questions raised by nandrolone testing. The committee concluded that testing methods were sound, but stated that athletes could be at risk from poorly labelled or **contaminated** vitamin or mineral supplements.

More or less?

A debate is raging as to whether there should be more or less drugs testing and whether more or fewer substances should be banned. A majority of people feel that more testing is the only way to catch the drugs cheats and rid sports of doping. New drugs and ways of masking doping are being developed all the time. As a result, the list of prohibited substances and methods has to be reviewed regularly.

Another view is that banning fewer substances and concentrating instead on testing for the major, most harmful drugs is the only way the fight against drugs in sport can move forward. The anti-doping authorities are struggling because of the costs and sheer scale of testing so many people for so many different substances. Reducing the list of banned substances might make it possible to stamp out the most serious, harmful drugs in sports. It may also allow authorities to spend more time and money educating and counselling young athletes so that they do not start to use drugs in the first place.

"As soon as we give in to the notion that anything goes then the concept of fair competition has no meaning."

David Moorcroft, Chief of UK Athletics

British sprinter Linford Christie leaves court after winning his case on the taking of performance-enhancing drugs.

Save our sport

A small number of people in sport fear that they are fighting a losing battle, which may bankrupt their particular sport. They argue that the money required to fund testing and fight numerous court cases is only part of the cost. More testing may lead to their sport's most famous participants being banned. Further drugs scandals could cause **sponsors** to desert the sport and even lead the public to turn off and tune in to one of the many other sports competing for their attention.

Those who disagree say that sports organizations have a greater duty than simply to look after themselves. They claim that drugs carry health risks and damage people in society, and say that it is the duty of sports governing bodies to stamp out drug use. Campaigners against drug-taking in sport claim that if famous competitors use drugs, it is very important that they are seen to be punished, because they have an enormous influence over others.

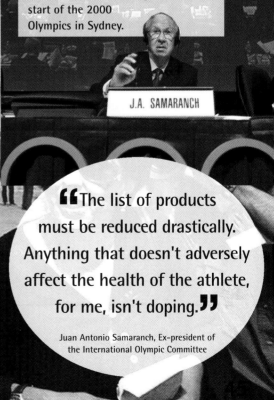

Ex-president of the International Olympics Committee, Juan Antonio Samaranch, at a meeting before the start of the 2000 Olympics in Sydney.

J.A. SAMARANCH

❝The list of products must be reduced drastically. Anything that doesn't adversely affect the health of the athlete, for me, isn't doping.❞

Juan Antonio Samaranch, Ex-president of the International Olympic Committee

Is it fair?

The whole concept of testing and banning athletes for doping has been called into question by a handful of people. A few argue that only less famous athletes are picked on and that sports authorities would not dare to catch and ban a major star. The cases of Ben Johnson and Linford Christie prove that this is not true.

Part of the reason that drugs are banned is that they can give an athlete an unfair advantage. Some people ask: Is taking drugs any more unfair than certain other methods which are not available to everyone? For example, only some athletes can afford to train at high altitude to increase their **stamina**. In Christian Wolmar's book, *Drugs And Sport*, British doctor Richard Nicholson argues: 'The amount of unfairness introduced by drug-taking is no more than that of runners using **pacemakers** or a few athletes having access to advanced **physiological** and sports medicine laboratories while the majority do not.'

Many people disagree with what Nicholson says. They argue that some unfairness will always exist in sport, yet talent and dedication tend to reach the top. Doping is banned not just because it gives athletes an unfair advantage but because of health and other issues. Altitude training, employing the best coach or paying to see a medical specialist are not illegal or harmful to an athlete's health as many drugs can be. Nor are they likely to harm another person who is influenced to act in a similar way.

But what about the fact that different sports have different rules? Is it fair that a weightlifter can be banned for using **steroids**, while in US major league baseball there is, as yet, no ban on steroid use? The answer is probably no, but perhaps what is needed here is for those sports lagging behind to catch up. Authorities like **WADA** and other groups are campaigning hard to get agreements across all sports. After many years of resistance, major league baseball may introduce testing for steroids in future seasons. A June 2002 survey of 556 baseball professionals saw 79 per cent supporting independent testing for steroid use.

In the end, whatever the problems raised by drugs testing, many drug-free athletes see testing as a necessary part of high-performance sport. Testing is not only there to catch cheats, it is also there to protect the reputation of those athletes who compete fairly and cleanly.

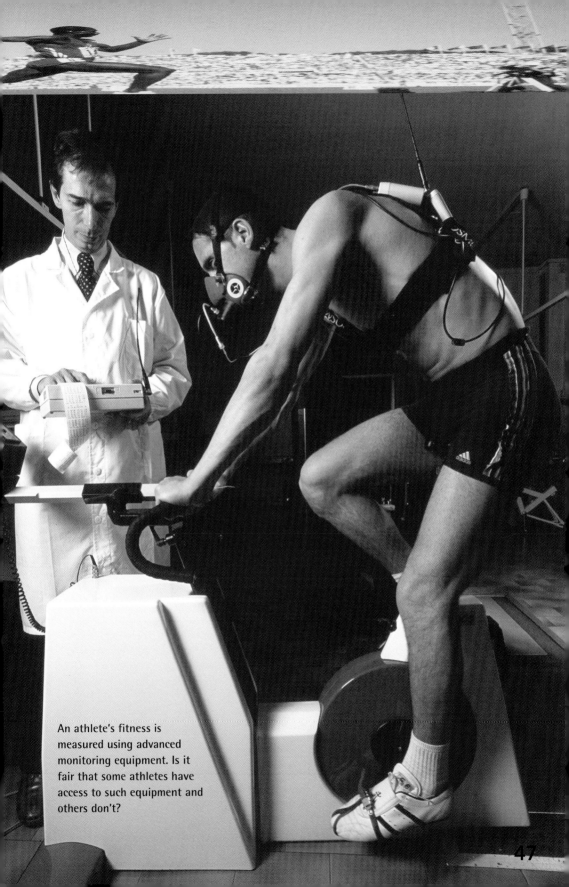

An athlete's fitness is measured using advanced monitoring equipment. Is it fair that some athletes have access to such equipment and others don't?

Doping and young athletes

Three friends enjoy a game of soccer. Sport is much more fun and rewarding when it is enjoyed free from drugs.

Drugs in sport can kill and injure. Taking drugs breaks the rules of most sports and can lead to you being barred from taking part in the sport you enjoy. In addition, owning, using or passing drugs on to others is often a criminal offence.

At some point in their sporting careers, all young athletes will experience the pressure to succeed and the disappointment of losing. But the important thing is not to allow these pressures to push you into taking drugs.

Sport is about trying to be the very best, but doing so fairly without breaking the rules. Taking drugs robs you of the pride and satisfaction of competing well. Drug taking can upset your family, friends and team-mates and can cause you physical and mental harm.

The true greats of sport have avoided doping. They include past legends like Michael Jordan and Carl Lewis as well as current stars such as David Beckham, Tiger Woods, Ian Thorpe and Venus and Serena Williams. To get to the top in

"When I was a kid I dreamed of becoming the best. Drugs kill dreams. It's just not worth it."

Serena Williams, US tennis star

sport you need talent, skill and huge amounts of training and dedication. You do not need drugs. As professional baseball player Barry Larkin says, 'Pills or powders don't replace hard work.'

You can help to keep drugs out of sport by resisting taking drugs in all situations, even if you are put under pressure to fit in with your group or team. By staying drug-free you are helping to set an example to others. It is never a good idea to cover up for someone who you know is on drugs or who offers drugs to you. It is much better for your sport if the problem is brought out into the open.

Use the reference section at the back of this book to learn more about specific issues, but do not stop there if you have further questions. Speak to your teachers, coaches and parents. You can also contact the organization that runs your sport. Sports organizations often provide information packs and direct advice on issues connected to drugs and sport.

Facts and figures

Drug use

The 1999 US Healthy Competition Foundation survey found that 71% of young people and 76% of adults say that they are less likely to watch Olympic sports if they know that the athletes are using drugs.

In the US National Household Survey on Drug Abuse (2000), 61% of all twelve to seventeen year-olds had participated in team sports during the previous year. 8.1% of those who participated in team sports reported **illicit** drug use as opposed to 12.2% of those who did not play sport.

In the 2000 US Monitoring the Future survey, 18.9% of 19–22 year-olds surveyed reported having a friend who was a current user of **steroids**.

A poll of 556 professional baseball players conducted by USA TODAY magazine in June, 2001 found 89% believe there is some steroid use in the game, 10% believe more than half of their peers are users and 44% feel pressure to use steroids to compete.

In a Council of Europe Survey of athletes in 33 countries, the banned drugs and methods used by athletes were **anabolic steroids** (39%), **stimulants** (32%), **marijuana** (12%), **narcotic analgesics** (4.6%), refusal of testing (3.8%), **diuretics** (3.2%), **blood doping** (1.1%), **local anaesthetics** (0.9%) and **beta-blockers** (0.4%).

An International Olympic Committee study surveyed 2200 US college students at eleven different colleges. Around 6% of male and 1% of female athletes used steroids regularly. The highest rate of use was in football and track and field.

Drug testing

Numbers of drug tests conducted at Summer Olympics

1968 Mexico City	1968
1972 Munich	2079
1976 Montreal	786
1980 Moscow	645
1984 Los Angeles	1507
1988 Seoul	1598
1992 Barcelona	1848
1996 Atlanta	1923
2000 Sydney	2758

UK drugs test totals and positive results

The figures below show the total number of tests carried out in a year and the number of positive results found.

1993/94	3901	48
1994/95	4365	78
1995/96	4327	89
1996/97	4458	90
1997/98	4577	79
1998/99	5144	76
1999/00	6133	119
2000/01	5368	110
2001/02	5954	101

Source: UK Sport (formerly known as the United Kingdom Sports Council)

Australian drugs test totals and positive results

The figures below show the total number of tests carried out in a year and the number of positive results found.

1989/90	1272	54
1990/91	2656	76
1991/92	2444	40
1992/93	2877	52
1993/94	2802	38
1994/95	3108	33
1995/96	3296	34
1996/97	3499	35
1997/98	4313	36
1998/99	4801	43
1999/00	5745	34
2000/01	6194	22

Source: Australian Sports Drug Agency (ASDA)

New Zealand drugs test totals and positive results

The figures below show the total number of tests carried out in a year and the number of positive results found.

1994/95	664	8
1995/96	666	8
1996/97	660	11
1997/98	994	16
1998/99	951	6
1999/00	1180	11

Source: New Zealand Sports Drug Agency (NZSDA)

Further information

International organizations

World Anti-Doping Agency (WADA)
www.wada-ama.org

International Olympic Committee (IOC)
www.olympic.org

Contacts in the UK and Ireland

Department for Culture, Media & Sport
Sport and Recreation Division
2–4 Cockspur Street
London SW1Y 5DH
Tel: 020 7211 6000
www.culture.gov.uk

The National Sports Medicine Institute of the United Kingdom
32 Devonshire Street
London W1G 6PX
Tel: 020 7251 0583
www.nsmi.org.uk

UK Sport
Drug-Free Sport Directorate
40 Bernard St
London WC1N 1ST
Tel: 020 7211 5129
email: drug-free@uksport.gov.uk
Drug Information Line: 0800 528 0004
www.uksport.gov.uk/did

Sport England
Sport England
16 Upper Woburn Place
London WC1H 0QP
Tel: 020 7273 1500
www.sportengland.org

Sportscotland
Caledonia House
South Gyle
Edinburgh EH12 9DQ
Tel: 0131 317 7200
www.sportscotland.org.uk

The Sports Council for Northern Ireland
House of Sport
Upper Malone Road,
Belfast, BT9 5LA
Tel: 028 9038 1222
www.sportni.net

The Sports Council for Wales
Head Office
Sophia Gardens
Cardiff, CF11 9SW
Tel: 029 2030 0500
www.sports-council-wales.co.uk

Irish Sports Council
21 Fitzwilliam Square
Dublin 2
Ireland
Tel: (+353) 1 240 7700
www.irishsportscouncil.ie

Concerted Action in the Fight against Doping in Sport (CAFDIS)
Suite 35
Blackrock Clinic
Blackrock
Co. Dublin
Ireland
www.cafdis-antidoping.net

Contacts in the USA and Canada

United States Anti-Doping Agency (USADA)
1265 Lake Plaza Drive
Colorado Springs
Colorado 80906
Tel: 719 785 2000
email: webmaster@usantidoping.org
www.usantidoping.org

United States Olympic Committee
Colorado Springs Olympic Training Center
National Headquarters
One Olympic Plaza
Colorado Springs
CO 80909
www.usolympicteam.com

The Healthy Competition Foundation
PO Box 81289
Chicago
IL 60681-0289
email: healthycompetition@bcbsa.com
www.healthycompetition.org

The American Council for Drug Education
164 West 74th Street
New York, NY 10023
Fax: 212.595.2553
www.acde.org

National Institute on Drug Abuse
6001 Executive Blvd.
Bethesda
MD 20892-9561
www.steroidabuse.org

Canadian Center for Ethics in Sport
2197 Riverside Drive, Suite 202
Ottawa, Ontario K1H 7X3
Tel: 613 521-3340
www.cces.ca

Contacts in Australia and New Zealand

Australian Sports Drug Agency (ASDA)
PO Box 345
Curtin ACT 2605
Tel: (+61) 02 6206 0200
email: asda@asda.org.au
www.asda.org.au

Australian Sports Drug Testing Laboratory
www.agal.gov.au/ASDTL

Australian Institute of Sport
PO Box 176
Belconnen
ACT 2616
Tel: (+61) 02 6214 1111
www.ais.org.au/

New Zealand Sports Drug Agency
PO Box 18339
Auckland
Tel: (+64) 9521 5706 or 0800 drugfree
email: nzsda@nzsda.co.nz
www.nzsda.co.nz

Glossary

acne
outbreak of pimples, found particularly on the face, neck, chest and back

addictive
causing someone to form a habit that they cannot give up

amphetamine
manufactured drug that is a powerful stimulant, affecting the brain and central nervous system

anabolic steroid
substance that adds bulk to muscles and increases strength

analgesic
drug such as aspirin that reduces the pain felt by a person

beta-blocker
drug that slows the human heartbeat

black market
illegal trade in something, such as drugs

blood doping
injecting of blood or parts of blood into an athlete to improve their performance

cocaine
strong stimulant drug made from the coca plant

Commonwealth Games
sports competition involving 72 nations with historical links to the UK

contaminated
made impure

creatine
substance produced by the body, which can help store energy for muscles

decathlete
athlete who takes part in the decathlon, which consists of ten running, jumping and throwing events

dehydration
loss of water from the body

dependence
overpowering feeling of need for a particular drug

deterrent
something that puts people off

diuretic
drug that removes water from the body

enhance
to increase or improve something

ephedrine
drug that acts as a stimulant on a person's nervous system

gladiator
ancient Roman warrior who fought against other gladiators or against fierce animals

haemoglobin
substance found in red blood cells that carries oxygen from the lungs to the muscles and other parts of the body

hashish
brownish-black solid made from the cannabis plant

heptathlon
athletics competition for women, that consists of seven running, jumping and throwing events

heroin
addictive, illegal drug made from a particular kind of poppy plant

hormone
substance produced in one part of the body and carried in the blood, which affects how body organs such as the heart or brain operate

illicit
illegal, or against the law

local anaesthetic
substance that creates a temporary loss of feeling in part of the body

LSD
powerful drug that can distort the way someone feels, hears, sees, smells and thinks. The initials stand for lysergic acid diethylamide.

marijuana
dried leaves and stalks of the cannabis plant

masking agent
substance that has the effect of hiding another substance

methadone
type of narcotic analgesic that is sometimes used as a substitute for heroin or morphine

morphine
type of narcotic analgesic made from a particular poppy plant, which is sometimes used to treat people in severe pain, but is banned from use in sport

nandrolone
type of anabolic steroid that is banned by most sports

narcotic analgesics
powerful painkilling drugs, including heroin and morphine, which can be addictive and can cause serious health problems

nervous system
system of cells, tissues, and organs that carries messages to and from the brain

ovaries
female reproductive organs that create and store eggs

pacemaker
athlete who does not compete in a race, but who helps others keep at a certain speed for part of the race

performance-enhancing drugs
drugs that help a sportsperson to train harder or play better in some way

physiological
to do with the body

positive drugs test
test that shows an athlete to have banned substances in their body that are above the allowed limit

prescription
order for a drug or a medicine signed by a doctor or a trained medical officer

recreational drugs
drugs, such as alcohol and cannabis, which are sometimes used in social groups and in leisure situations

sanctions
punishments that are dealt out when rules or laws are broken

sponsors
private companies or individuals who use their money to promote sports or athletes

stamina
ability to keep performing at close to maximum effort for a period of time

steroid
see **anabolic steroid**

stimulant
drug that stimulates the heart, brain or nervous system

strychnine
drug made from the seeds of a South Asian tree, which can act as a stimulant but is mainly used today as a form of poison

testicles
oval-shaped male reproductive organs housed in a pouch called the scrotum and found at the base of the penis

testosterone
main male hormone that helps create male sex characteristics, including body hair and increased muscle growth

tolerance
way in which the human body reduces its response to a set amount of a drug

WADA
World Anti-Doping Agency, an international organization set up to fight illegal drugs in sport

Index

Titles in the *Just the Facts* series include:

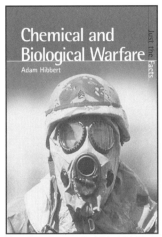

Hardback   0 431 16160 7

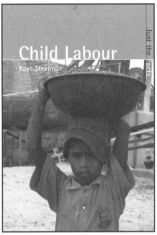

Hardback   0 431 16161 5

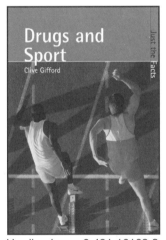

Hardback   0 431 16162 3

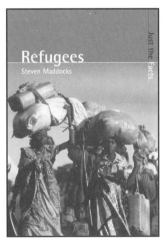

Hardback   0 431 16163 1

Hardback   0 431 16164 X

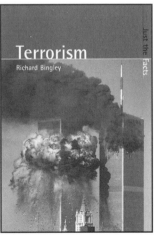

Hardback   0 431 16165 8

Find out about the other titles in this series on our website www.heinemann.co.uk/library